A Tree with a Knee

Written and photographed by
Virginia Sands

To Kelly
with love and
gratitude

Virginia Sands

Diamond Clear Vision

Come with me
down this
magical path.
Surprises are
waiting every
step of the way.

Oh, look,
can it be?
Don't be silly...
a tree with a knee?

Look up above.
Tiny yellow porcupines
are swinging on a twig.

Shhh!
It's a sleeping dog
with his head
on the leaves.

Look who's marching up the hill...
thousands of turkeys.
What a thrill!

9

Is that a clamshell stuck on a tree?
How did it get so far from the sea?

Little copper bells hanging on a tree...

only fairy breezes can play their melody.

Up from the murky, muddy swamp
climbs this funny fellow.

Don't you worry, don't be scared...
he's really very mellow.

Hidden in the
leafy woods
a tipi hugs
the ground.
Chipmunks scurry
through the door
to take a look around.

Bristly, stickly
tickly brush
shimmering,
shining
sparkling hush.

It's the wispy, wavy woods people gathering for a meeting.

15

Bang!

Boom!

Crackle!

Exploding in
the sky
fireworks and
rockets for
the Fourth
of July.

16

Soft glowing light from a candle lit pine.

Two rosy slippers
are caught
on a plant.

Someone's green mitten
is hanging on a tree.

Look! Is it a marble
or a shiny bouncy ball?

Looks like an alien mask...but where is its mouth?

A stately ship is waiting to cruise out to sea...

...and a lumpy, bumpy turtle watches to see when it will leave.

Quick, look over there...
a swirly bird is fleeing across the sifting sand.

What have we here?
A miniature ship is grounded on the shore.

Down by the river, oh what a sight,

the ghosts are out swimming on Halloween night.

A spooky ghost
is floating
through the
frozen
winter woods.

Frozen to a twig,
an icy caterpillar
waits for spring.

When soft spring comes
to melt the icy blue,
the tiny woodland people
will ride in this canoe.

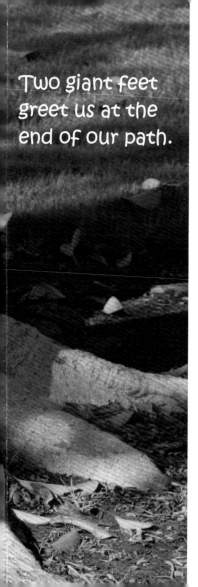

Two giant feet greet us at the end of our path.

There are many secret paths waiting for us to explore.

Key to Photographs